T0381419

Holy Horrors of Thy Heart

SCARLET MARIE

Contents

ISBN: Softcover   978-1-9845-4896-2
        Hardcover   978-1-9845-4894-8
        EBook   978-1-9845-4895-5

Print information available on the last page.

Rev. date: 08/31/2018

To order additional copies of this book, contact:
Xlibris
1-888-795-4274
www.Xlibris.com
Orders@Xlibris.com

Chapter 1

Dying Rose

MAGIC MIRROR

Mirror, Mirror, on the wall, who's the vainest man of all?

Mirror, Mirror, on the wall, who believes his wit surpasses them all?

Wit is raw . . . He'll have to fall,

Fall from grace . . . It's like if he was laced,

Laced by drugs, or laced from up above.

Cloud nine, he wanted all her time,

To reflect, he'll spend his dimes . . . Dimes and dollars just to see majestic, true beauty.

Beauty is pain, filled with shame.

He thought he could win this game.

Wit, it's raw. She stands tall.

Tall, tall tale of a man who thought he would prevail.

Beauty is beast. She'll never let him sleep,

Sleep alone, or sleep with clones . . . Clones of the beautiful beast he once uncovered,

It took him forty years just to discover.

She raped and ravished, maimed his name

Cast his ego down with pain

Gates of hell, do your spell. Heed this man, lest he recover

Lover's delight. Her wit is bright

Devil, some say you're the angel of light

Light him up . . . He and his mother

Your lover left and rediscovered

Blessed with beauty, blessed with rest

Magic Mirror, help me test. Test their hearts, and test mine too,

Magic Mirror, may I pass through?

RED WOMAN

Devilish woman, she fights for my soul,
Face-to-face oppressions her goal,
I tendered her my heart, my home, and my goals,
Woman in red; woman I wed,
Till death do us part, the begging I dread,
Lord, let this witch of a bitch surrender to my kiss,
Reverse the twist of her hips and the warm spit that drips,
She has my making decisions ever so sick,

Red Woman, I love you. Your magic I'll miss,
It's filthy rich . . . My prayer is this:

Lift not your spell; possess me once more,
The child you bore remain our core.
Blood of my bones, my house remains your home,
Woman and rib, without you, I can't.

BIG BAD WOLF

Eighteen years old, feeling daring and bold,

Big bad wolf wants to eat me up,

Big bad wolf wants to free me up,

Freedom of speech; I whisper his dreams,

Freedom to fuck, my face and my guts,

Salacious lover, he ravished me all over the covers,

Blankets and pillows, lotion and lace,

My new favorite place,

Time to escape,

He whispers my name,

Name me Bunny, name me Love,

Name me Wife . . . if you want to consume my life!

DEVIL IN DISGUISE

You remind me of the Devil in disguise.

I met him once,

You and he have similar eyes.

Mr. Devil, Mr. Daddy, Mr. Man King, close your eyes,

They betray you...Again this time.

I meet him twice,

We fucked all night.

Now each and every night he holds me tight,

He holds me down.

Look at me now...Hell bound!

We're on third round,

Daddy I'm still down.

Devil in disguise, she learned from your crafty little lies.

You met her once...Small dark eyes.

You meet her twice...she stole your life.

Isn't that the title wife?

BLACK BIRD

He eats my love, calls me his dove,
Pure and pretty, angel in white,
Lie him down, turn out the lights,
Unzip my feathers as he closes his eyes,
He's love drunk and high,
Ms. Mary, I'm scary when I turn off the lights,
I find feathers . . . Yet they're not white,

Blacker than night, and red are my eyes. Horns that adorn, and candles that cry,
Crazy in love; a blind man and a dove,
Dove is delight, but a raven wins the fight,
He fights on his back, sedated and trusting,
Blackest of hearts, I'll dress for the part,
For white steals the heart, but black steals the soul . . .
I'll mascaraed beauty; gentle, yet bold,

Lust is what I feed him . . . Me and Ms. Mary
Now that he's sedated, I won't be so scary,
Black beauty. Black magic. Black bird; and my name is his favorite dirty word.

FOOLISH MAN

My wicked tongue, my dirty mouth, my bitter heart; it's my best art
Fooled by love. Confused by doubt
You never could turn this woman out

My toxic spit seeps in your mouth
Through your blood, then back through mine
I have only time. Time to kill. Time to steal. Time to thrill. Time to chill,
Chill my heart, and freeze it . . . right
Right or wrong, it's been too long
Long live our love. Long live our rage
 What do we do besides age
Age with grace or age with waste . . . Waste of a good marriage,

You wanted life. I wanted strife
My sickness subsides
You are wise. Wise to let go. Wise to be bold
Wise, wife . . . And there she goes
Foolish man, you had no plan . . . My sorcerous soul stole your toll
Foolish man, you let me know
Your wicked bitch . . . I fucked you sick,
Now say your prayers . . . one for you . . . and two for me
Foolish man, you'll crave my spit

ITCH

He only loves me in the bed.
I really get him red,
Like fire from the pit.
The burns turn to an itch.
It's how our souls stay glitched.

He's always there, running his hand through my hair,
Kissing my torso with that beauty stare,
My hot spot on his beard. Poison, trickling down his throat . . .
And my antidote of hope.

Lights on, fire out . . . Itch, itch, itch!
Eyes open wide, the irony of pride.
He loves me in the bed. Now, I get him water and fed.
So many demands, so many commands.
I'm tired.
Let's go back to bed; it's starting to itch,
You should really fuck this bitch.
Put her poison down your throat; she'll take yours with hope.
She only loves you in the bed . . .
After that, you always *itch*.

THERMOSTAT

He sets me a blaze and then pulls away,
To watch me shiver in my wrath,
The beauty of our thermostat,

Subconscious fire deep within, burn our hearts as we pretend,
Pretend angels, doves, and dew,
Pretend spring in a blizzard so cold.

BIRTHDAY

January 5, 2018, 3:25 p.m.
Feeling like I'm walking on water. Stomach full of butterflies

January 5, 2018, 4:25 p.m.
Drowning in a river of tears

My birthday wish: his presence dismissed.

THIRTEEN SEASONS

Life's a script, and so I cry. The love story bloody and gory
Thirteen seasons without reasons. Reasons of riddles; us kids and our fiddles
Play for Mom, and pray for Dad
Season 7, we all went mad
Mad mother, gluten father, suicidal son, me—the daughter with a gun
Fully loaded; I had my parents demoted
Down to Hades's house. Looks like Mother lost her blouse
Dad is thirsty; Mom's breasts must nurse he

Life's a script. Dad's the star. Mom, direct your series of horror
Season finale: a tragic, a trophy
Imagination of Mommy—abrasive, hormonal
Character of Father—oblivious and dumb
Staring the children, who eventually go numb

Practice makes perfect. The act must continue
With hick ups and hits . . . This show you can't miss
We all know these skits are silly and sick

GAME IS GAME

Leo served her papers of pain. Ink of shame engraved their names,
Heartache awaits. The game is game.
If only he were tame, exotic, and vain.
In vain, they lay. With others, they play. She played the victim . . . a villain delayed.

The papers bleed, and then they feed. Feed with hate, sex, and grapes.
She served him in youth and bore him his fruit.
Their loins lay with his pride's name.

The Leo, who can tame?
Vindictive lover, lion enraged,
She the goat, pretty little prey.

Stubborn goat, you are the host,
Host of horns; harlot don't morn.
Play her flute to seduce for truce.

Man will heed, ensnare the beast.
He'll take the bait; her horns don't break.
Man will heed lion's defeat.

Goat, be gallant. Goat, have glory. Goat, climb graciously; you'll eventually reign it.
For goat can't fight, but ambitions take flight.
Goat, you are goddess anointed . . . This is his horror story
Lion beheaded; woman declared it . . .

Chapter 2
Belittled Hearts

RING POP

I fucked him good. He knew I would.
I sucked him good. I knew I should
Seal the deal, save the date!
From me, this man shall not escape.

His mother's mad. I stole her man.
Man, she raised to lend his hands . . .
His hands I hold, his pockets too.

Mother-in-law, you look confused.
I guess you should not have been so crude.

Classy lady. Sassy lady. 3-karat; and baby, I swear it.
I fucked him good just like I should.

Ring pop, ring rock,
His pants just dropped. My wallet on top!

MOCKINGBIRD

I can't live without my mocking man

He claims I'm sexy when I'm mad

Runs up bills to give me chills

My mockingbird, mockingjay

Mimic me; sing and pray

Come now, honey,

Lights out . . . Slay

MY LOVE IS LOUD

On the day I wed, my grandmother took me by the hands, and she said,
"It is written: Love is patient. Love is kind; it does not envy. Love does not boast, nor is it proud,
Etcetera, etcetera, etcetera . . .

But Grandmother, my love is . . . My love is *loud*!
Jealous, easily angered, self-seeking, and record keeping . . . But this is how I keep him aroused,

My love is frail and torments like hell. His love is haughty; he literally burns my soul through my body.

Grandmother, this you may pray: Preserve my passion, preserve my days,
Preserve his crave,

No need to ransom . . . his heart he gave!

DISAPPOINT

I fuckin' love him. I adore him and only him.
I see him in my dreams—sad and mad, I never can appease.
Why? Why?
Why can't I relinquish what he needs?
Why do I fall, so fuckin' short?

Disappoint, disappoint, disappoint, times ten,
If he lets me, I'll do it ten times ten
We used to be best friends, and now the love of my life says we must end.

Mind over matter; may his seeds no longer scatter.
Going mad, I wish his heart sad.
Wish him in a fairy tale that will end in my prevail.

Disappoint me, disappoint me, disappoint me,
And so I squeeze; squeeze his heart . . .
My baby bleed.
I fuckin' love him . . . and now I can increase.

BEAUTY

Behold her beauty—majestic, unruly
Captivating lips; firm, sweet hips
His honey's thighs make sweeter than homemade pies

He wed her young
Her life just begun
They thought her dull. They thought her dumb
Since then, she's made those motherfuckers run
Run from flames, her torch did strain

Blame the beauty. Blame the bold
His heartless bliss; sensational woman of abyss

Her hands spun gold, while others too busy complaining of what she stole
And what do you know? Sarcastic laughter . . . Her hands spin faster

WASTE

Highs and lows. Love and hate. Hot and cold.
Why did I waste? My blood, my age, face, body, and mind,
Because I was blind. Blind in my mind's eye,
Blind by the blood before my eyes . . .

She is gorgeous. She is great. A daughter, we birthed in hate.
Do I stay and stay and stay until her big day?
No. Walk away, empty and depleted, but walk away before I ruin away.
My demise was and is, but will I rise,

Rise above the high . . . Evolve and beget beauty,
Beauty of the mind, body, and soul.
Whole, pure, and abundant.
Walk into a new faith of fire and love. Love me, myself, I
Less I die from soiled hate . . . No, that'll be his final fate.
Broken Spirit, I will rise. Broken Spirit, you tell lies.
Down is down; but up is high.
I will rise unto the highest sky. A star will glisten before my eyes.

Daughter, you were worth the pain I paved.
Your father was right; mother's true delight.
Waste not away. Lift your spirit. Shine so bright.
Thank your father. He got your anatomy right.
Our biggest fan—obsessed with me, in love with you.
Shine so bright because he put out my light.

DARK ANGEL

Death, Death, Death, do you hear me?

I'm calling again and again. Why have you forsaken me?

Why is my heart still throbbing?

Death, collect my bones,

Collect my soul, send me home.

This man, he torchers me in my home, in my mind, in my body . . . to my soul.

Death, it hurts . . .

Please, let me go to the other side,

Where there's no crying, no lying.

Death, I'm fuckin' dying, slow and distasteful,

Please come . . . Send my dark angel!

Chapter 3

Bond of Distaste

DIVORCE AND DEVIL

Divorce and devil, lie with me. Come, let's fantasize an erotic being

Solace my cries with your pack of lies

Divorce, you are our man. Devil, she is vain.

The two of you come with pleasure and pain.

He lies to me. She lies through me.

The ravens circle around my house . . . Deep desire to pluck my eyes out.

Eyes of a wife, mother, and daughter who once looked at her heavenly father

She made me do it; she always does.

He stalks my house with his covetous love.

Murderous maid, you lost his trust. Love doesn't live here anymore. Once divorce makes you his whore.

Divorce and devil, come set me free . . . For you have always fancied us three.

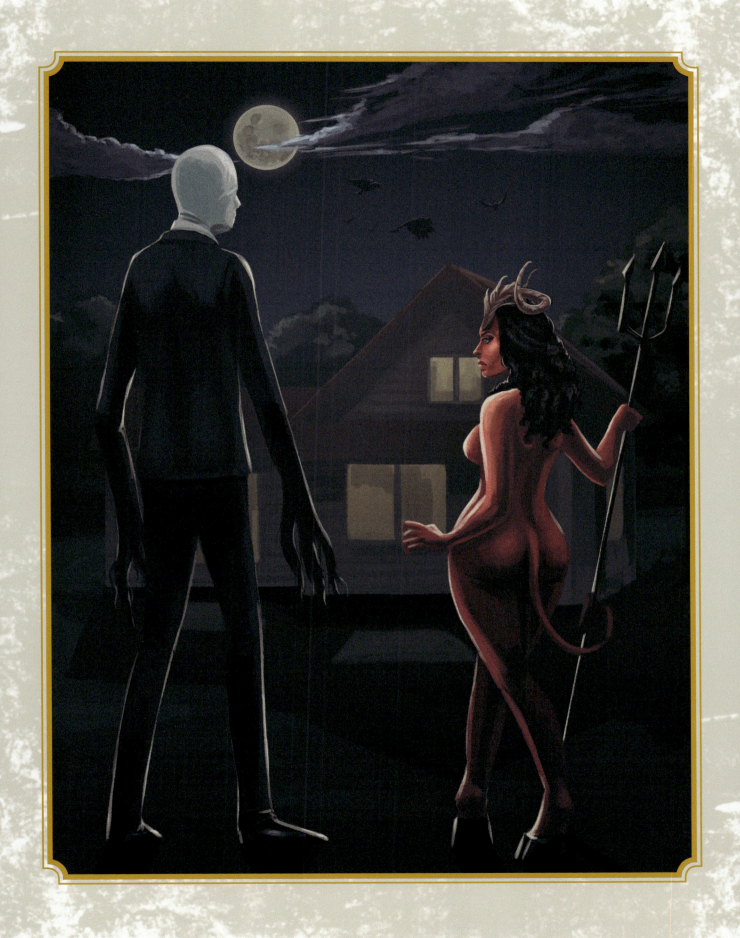

FINANCIAL FREEDOM

Financial freedom, we held a glimpse. Resemblance of a rainbow
Scent of a forest covered in dew. Fresh, clean, and forthcoming

Financial freedom, I once met you; before my husband gambled and played
Now I had to make acquaintance with foreclosures, BKs, IRS liens, and BOE bad dreams

And every chance he gets, he puts us right back in debt
Financial freedom, a fictional dream; I wake up in the middle of the night and silently scream

But you can't keep a good woman down . . . It's pound for pound
And husband, you won't win these later rounds

Financial freedom smells like rain and feels like fame; and yes, I'm sure it'll cure the pain

Gamble away, see if I stay . . . You lose either way

FIGHT

Dark deity, thrust through me
Rock me good . . . Like only you could
Dark deity, hold me tight; it's trying to fight
I want the light, it's half past night
Soothe me with your lullabies
Before I start to reckon why
Lull me to sleep, when I awake, I'll make them Break

Lord of light, lord of love, please help me
Fight the night

DANCE WITH YOUR DRAGONS

Children of God you claim to be. However, your aura is diseased
Dark and dirty, foulest smell
Smell of brimstone, reeks out of your mouth
They come in the name of Jesus as a changed child
Child of God they confess to be
The god of the underworld, unfortunately

Quench their thirst and listen to them rehearse
Sing and chant, swaying smoothly to that filthy dance
Dance with dragons . . . Yes, they do
Black sand, dreams; their father makes them shake, shiver, and scream
Black and blue, he plays them for fools
A fool in love, they yearn for his drugs
Hand them money. Hand them love. Better yet, hand them luck

Life's been hard for those they love
Front-row seats to witness the ferocious beast
The beast claimed you, and you claimed he
You danced and swayed so effortlessly

The ball will retire, and your guest will conspire,
Conspire your offspring before you sacrifice them to the dungeon of fire
Dance alone. Dance at a distance . . .
Dance with your dragon; he always listens

FAVORED BY GOD

Redundant relatives beg and gripe,
Borrow in sorrow. Swear to pay back tomorrow.

"Land of the free; home of the brave," that I claimed,
Born to two addicts—present and absent,
Government living . . . Now government giving,
I made it out . . . That I never did doubt.
I claimed my future, fortune, and fate.

Look to the left. Look to the right.
 And all I see are handouts . . . *Why?*
It's always the addicts, complainers, and haters
Assuming we owe them some special favor.

Favored by God; yes, I am
'Cause I got off my ass and harvest my plans.
So put down your hands and pull up your sleeves,
Or start living within your little means . . .
These are *my greens . . . You know what I mean!*

HALLELUJAH WHORES

Does the church take score?
Hallelujah whores, they never look nervous,
During Sunday's service.
Saturday night they fornicate with multiple mates,
Bedroom pastures . . . She breeds with sheep . . . And then she sleeps,

All the while; hallelujah sighs and amen as replies!

Your savior forgives; so you say to yourself,
"This life I'm gonna live,"
"These tithes I'm gonna give. Serve my brothers, they make dear lovers,"

Hallelujah, amen; she only fucks 10 percent.
Spread them open legs and lips. Move those hips,
Dip, dip, drip,

Cleanse your house. Fall to your knees; confess your sins . . . And hypocrisy *grins*,
Retreat, repeat, we sleep . . . Poor little sheep.

FAKE CRY

She molests my mind and edifies her crimes,
Crimes against scripture, she and hypocrisy were birthed as twin sisters
Her jaws swim open, deep abyss . . . The flames consume she and her kids
Shut her mouth. Shut her eyes. Shut her under the ground . . . And fake cry

Chapter 4

Limited Pleasure

NEW LOVER

New lover in my life; new lover, get it right

Right before our eyes, you'll see. The most sacred part of me

Fill my mouth with dirty lines

This fruit is ripe—ripe off the vine

Eat it fast, or eat it slow

I want to know—know how good you fill

Say your name with pleasure's pain. Scream and shout but don't pull out

Kitty, kitty, cum now play

Let's make today our favorite day

Day of darkness in the light. How I want to trust and bite

Smoke me out before my wine

And then again, a few more times

Spread me wide, then stand me up. Watch me smile as I blush

Head rush, highs; I love his sighs

This is the most unnatural lust

Lust for me as I lust for you

Love me good. I know you could

GAME CHANGE

Pillow talk, pillow text. Idle time, idle crime.

I read your text. Read your secrets. Read your lies; and then I knew it.
I said, "Fuckin' screw it." He'll read my face. He'll read my gaze.

I walked out and left him dazed: pillow talk, pillow play . . .

Now on his pillow, he prays . . . Game change . . . in idle, I lay.

MR. JONES

You have a missus. I have a master. Mr. Jones, you better deal faster.

Ecstasy, wet is we. You and I sexually fathom future fantasies.
Taboo, who? Not you, nor I.
You and I attempt to produce the most passionate fruit,
Fruit for the gods; we fuck against all odds,

Missus and master pushed us to laughter.
Laughter of love. Laughter of lust. Laughter of loss . . . Loss of our loyalty,
Lost in society.

Mr. Jones, my master's not home.
Tell the missus you're going out for some business.

BLOUSE

He came in my mouth and a little on my blouse.

He tastes just like heaven. His hands felt like hell.

Hot and haughty, how he makes me so naughty.

He burns my body, my soul, and my brain.

Let me explain; his cum feels like rain.

He thrusts just like thunder and lights me aflame.

The storm, the fight, to not do what's right,

Wrong is long . . . Hard, and sings songs,

Songs of moans. He groans, from his groins,

The seed he feeds has me bent on my knees.

Tears of rage, passion, and gain,

Gain him on my thighs once more. Gain him in my inner core,

This man; he fucks me like I'm his whore.

He has me begging for more and more.

PUSSYCAT

Pussycat, pussycat; Purr once relaxed
Cream of his crop; his semen on top
Taste of warm milk, taste of cream pie

Listen to my lion's eyes . . . and so I purr as reply

CLEANSING

Such a warm, cleansing climax
Face submerged with spit and grip
Grip and gaze, in my lips he lays
Kissing lips, kitty lips. Purge my lips
Calm me, claim me; baby, fuckin' tame me

You never cease to amaze me

LICK FOR LOVE

Lick his fingers. Lick his love,
He pulls them out, then smells his drug.
Drug him up,
Then drag them down . . . My panties fell straight to the ground
His late-night towel . . . Sniff the drug. Inhale, my love . . .
Baby, you're high and sprung . . .
Cum, let's lick for love.

DESK

Office table, office taste; fuck to the chase; no games I play.
Face to face, I breathe his whisky; he breathes my wine.
And then just like that . . . the perfect crime.
Wine, dine, and office time . . . Thanks for dinner. Thanks for drinks. Thanks for the desk where
My body was blessed.

BRAND-NEW

Messy hair; eyes smeared black. Lipstick gone, and earrings off,
Shoe is lost, her panties too.

He looks at her as if she was brand-new,
A new doll, a new Barbie, a new baby.

That look is priceless; price of appreciation, admiration . . . emancipation.
He looks at her, and she appears complete. That woman need not to compete.

Brand-new bedroom, brand-new toys. Just like children, life's simple joys.

SIN, SINCERELY

He let it seep as we did sleep. Sanctified, my heart did cry.
Cried for more just to explore . . . Explore the dangers of this drug.
This dose is given in his bed. Now all I want is to be wed.

Unification, I smell high. Unification, I drink dry.
Dry my mouth, its spilling out words they love to talk about.
Talk about my dirty deeds.
He loves my stories to proceed . . . Proceed with caution; no, not me,
I want it like Sin City . . . Sin with me. Sin in me. Sin, sincerely,

Rum and ice, I will entice
Pour you out, without a doubt,
Sprinkle, sprinkle, my drink twinkles.
Unionize a few more tries.
The night is young. We just begun,
Start it slow . . . Then let it grow . . . Grow with groans. He loves my moans.
I always tease him before I please him.
Please, please, talk about these dirty deeds . . . You have me on my hands and knees,
Married to our memories.

REY OF NIGHT

Cali king, my rey of night. Lay on pillows piled high,
My sense of smell, taste him well. Taste him deep, even in my sleep,

Drip and drool; I hope he's not playing me for a fool,
A fool in love, with oils he rubs . . .
First, we play; later, we pray. Pray we never tire, never lie,
Lay with others, why?
When we make each other high,

Hallucinate; as I sit upon his face,
Soaked and saturated, his tongue so sly
Poisoned pleasure; my rey eats clever,
Waters of love splish and splash,
He then bends me over and paddles my ass.

Devour my flower, devilish touch. I can't seem to blush,
I feel pure lust.
Swallow him whole, suck and cuss,
Words that disturb spill out of my brain. He's literally fucking me insane.

Inside out, eat and pout. Pout those lips and hold these hips,
Sip, sip, sip,
Daddy, you have an amazing grip.

BLUES

Break through blues. Baby, I'm screwed
Blue for life. 'Cause I could never be your wife,
Mr. Grand, Mr. Man,
Sweet and humble, he made my stomach rumble.

Patio passions: Me and Mr. Man. Candles, condoms, cannabis, and kiss
Kiss me soft with those big fat lips; eat me soft; savor our flavor
The flavor is high and never gets dry.

Outside, the moonlight soothes.
What a night it was—ever so bright, stars glisten.
And yes, they listened . . .
Listened and learned that lovers yearn,
Yearn for touch, taste, and smell . . . even if it leads to hell,

Lovers yearn for midnight moons,
The day is blue, a horrid hue,

Give me night, black-and-white. Hold me tight . . .
Break through blues; baby boo, I'm missing you.

Chapter 5

Left Handed Homemaker

ENLIGHTENED BEING

Enlightened being, I am a queen. Queen of Hearts, cause there's this tale.
It goes something like, "Love never fails."
Universe, bring me up, then sow me down,
On life's fickle ground, foundation bound,
Love can conquer. Yes, it can.
Foes and fans, I'm God's grand plan,
Watch me bleed, and then I'll lead.
Lead my life and forget about yesterday's strife.

Enlightened being, my heart should dream,
Life throws blows to whom she chose and then I rose . . .
Vanquished those that were opposed,
Conquered quest, and crushed the rest . . .
Remembered those who esteemed me best.

Queen of Hearts, enlightened being, look to your beautiful wings,
Guard them as you bend and bleed.
I must make haste; No time to face . . .
Queen of Hearts, we share a thing; we're both best blunt and love the hunt
Hunt for Help, and there she dwells,
In my heart, I guard her now . . .
Captive to my energies. Captive to a more powerful being,
Enlighten me . . . For I am queen.

GOD'S ADORN

I am woman, God's adorn. Hear me roar, watch me score
I am woman; heed my wings and watch me soar
I am woman; I am Eve, out of the garden on barefoot.

An angel appears and lends its wings. Suddenly, I know man's defeat.

I am woman; watch me soar.

Man, you resemble a bloodthirsty boar; the devil's had fun making you his whore.

CHOICE IS GOLD

We were born to love; we were born to lose,
In this day and age, we're able to choose,
Choose our lovers, choice of gold.
Choice is clear. Choice has time; need not scurry.
Millennials mingle; society now allows woman to indulge and be single.
Time is good. Time has taste.
Time our parents used to waste.
Waste not no more; my daughter, I adore.
The world is yours . . . Go out . . . Explore.

THROUGH THE WINDOWS OF MAN

Men are weak; and swayed by beauty.

Beauty is a faze and desperately deceitful; and yet through beauty and deceit,

Does a woman acquire favor?

"My god . . . What is to become of man?"

Woman will pluck man's power in effort to claim his throne.

Lest man pluck out his own weakness . . .

Through the windows of man will us women ascend,

Man, your reign,

 Is damn near end.

SHE IS FUTURE

Mary, Mary, marijuana . . . Married to our pre-Madonna
Legally, she undressed me; anticipate the consummate
Dancing diva, seductive sway. Color of love, color of life
Provocative; she will wife
Goddess divine, create new wine
Govern our minds; I'm told we live in perilous times
Remember about the native's plea. Remember 'bout slavery,
The times man cried; the times we died—died to self, a nation's drought
Newly born we will adorn
Green, green grass, I dreamed you last

Last night's session is in question
Religiously, we cannot be; so spiritually, engage with me
Blow their minds; it's voters' time
Some men judge, and others sigh
Comply with law; our rights stand tall
Vote you in and turn you out
Out and open, she had America chocken

She is future. She is free
She is gift, like Lady Liberty
A gift of healing. A gift of love
Divine lady fell from above
Raindrops water her with doves. Yes, she is the symbol of love

AMAZING YOU ARE

Western young woman, how lucky you are,
In this millennial life, you may reach for the stars.

Asian, Afro, Latin, and Caucasian, we persevered together and put up a fight.
A running woman, an Afro man; America the beautiful, God's perfect plan.

Commander-in-chief soon she will be,
Take us to the moon. Take us to Mars.
Show the world what Western women are,

We are daughters of dedication, birth by perseverance, baptized by assurance.

Western young woman, amazing you are.

NATIVE

Native American woman: Carmel, California
Father's side; father's pride

American Latina: Montclair, California
A native to this desert, a native to these states
So please, don't hate

FEELS FUCKIN' NICE

I have your man. I hold your man; your man holds me . . .

What did you expect? That he wouldn't marry me?

Did you expect us not to make it? After all, we did fall,

Fall in love, fall in life; and we did it twice. Feels fuckin' nice . . .

I hold my man against your plan.

One look at you, and he damn near ran.

HOLY HORROR OF MY HEART

Holy Horror we must now part.
My heroine and ex–best friend,
I'll leave you here, in black-and-white.
I must make haste to Wisdom's right.

Left is lonely, dark with gloom,
You and I shared many moons,
Make new lovers, make new friends.

Holy Horror remembers this:
You were my first love, my first friend, my first foe,
But I have to grow.

Sincerely, your ex–best friend,
I'll never forget you, oh heroine.

Extended Bio

Scarlet Marie is the eldest of four siblings. Her mother suffers from severe depression which lead Scarlet to host dual roles; as a young child she was both mother and sister. This extreme childhood lead her to a complex perspective on life's challenges and relationships. As new contemporary times prove prominent her aspects of family, love and spirituality is ever unfolding as she embraces a more selfish side; opposing the selfless family motto her mother and husband abruptly imposed. Holy Horrors of thy Heart is a dark compilation of emotions that liberate one's inner truths.

Printed in the United States
By Bookmasters